Superman and the Miserable, Rotten, No Fun, Really Bad Day

DAVE CROATTO

Illustrated by TOM RICHMOND

MAD BOOKS

William M. Gaines Founder
John Ficarra Senior VP & Executive Editor
Charlie Kadau, Joe Raiola, Dave Croatto Senior Editors
Jacob Lambert Associate Editor
Sam Viviano VP – Art & Design
Ryan Flanders Design Director
Patricia Dwyer Assistant Art Director
Bernard Mendoza Production Artist

ADMINISTRATION

Diane Nelson President
Dan DiDio Publisher
Jim Lee Publisher
Geoff Johns President & Chief Creative Officer
Amit Desai Executive VP – Business & Marketing Strategy, Direct to Consumer & Global Franchise Management
Sam Ades Senior VP & General Manager, Digital Services
Bobbie Chase VP & Executive Editor, Young Reader & Talent Development
Mark Chiarello Senior VP – Art, Design & Collected Editions
John Cunningham Senior VP – Sales & Trade Marketing
Anne DePies Senior VP – Business Strategy, Finance & Administration
Don Falletti VP – Manufacturing Operations
Lawrence Ganem VP – Editorial Administration & Talent Relations
Alison Gill Senior VP – Manufacturing & Operations
Hank Kanalz Senior VP – Editorial Strategy & Administration
Jay Kogan VP – Legal Affairs
Jack Mahan VP – Business Affairs
Nick J. Napolitano VP – Manufacturing Administration
Eddie Scannell VP – Consumer Marketing
Courtney Simmons Senior VP – Publicity & Communications
Jim (Ski) Sokolowski VP – Comic Book Specialty Sales & Trade Marketing
Nancy Spears VP – Mass, Book, Digital Sales & Trade Marketing
Michele R. Wells VP – Content Strategy

Superman created by Jerry Siegel and Joe Shuster
By special arrangement with the Jerry Siegel family

For Carter and Evan, from Dad

Published by MAD Books. An imprint of E.C. Publications, Inc.
1325 Avenue of the Americas, New York, NY 10019

A Warner Bros. Entertainment Company

Printed by Transcontinental Interglobe, Beauceville, QC, Canada. 9/8/17. First Printing.

ISBN: 978-1-4012-7611-9

Library of Congress Cataloging-in-Publication Data is available.

Though Alfred E. Neuman wasn't the first to say "A fool and his money are soon parted," here's your chance to prove the old adage right — subscribe to MAD! Simply call 1-800-4-MADMAG to order!

Visit MAD online at: www.madmagazine.com

When my alarm went off this morning, I hit "snooze" too hard and broke my phone. Then I got out of bed and stepped right on my glasses. And I realized that I must have sleep-walked during the night. I could tell it was going to be a miserable, rotten, no fun, really bad day.

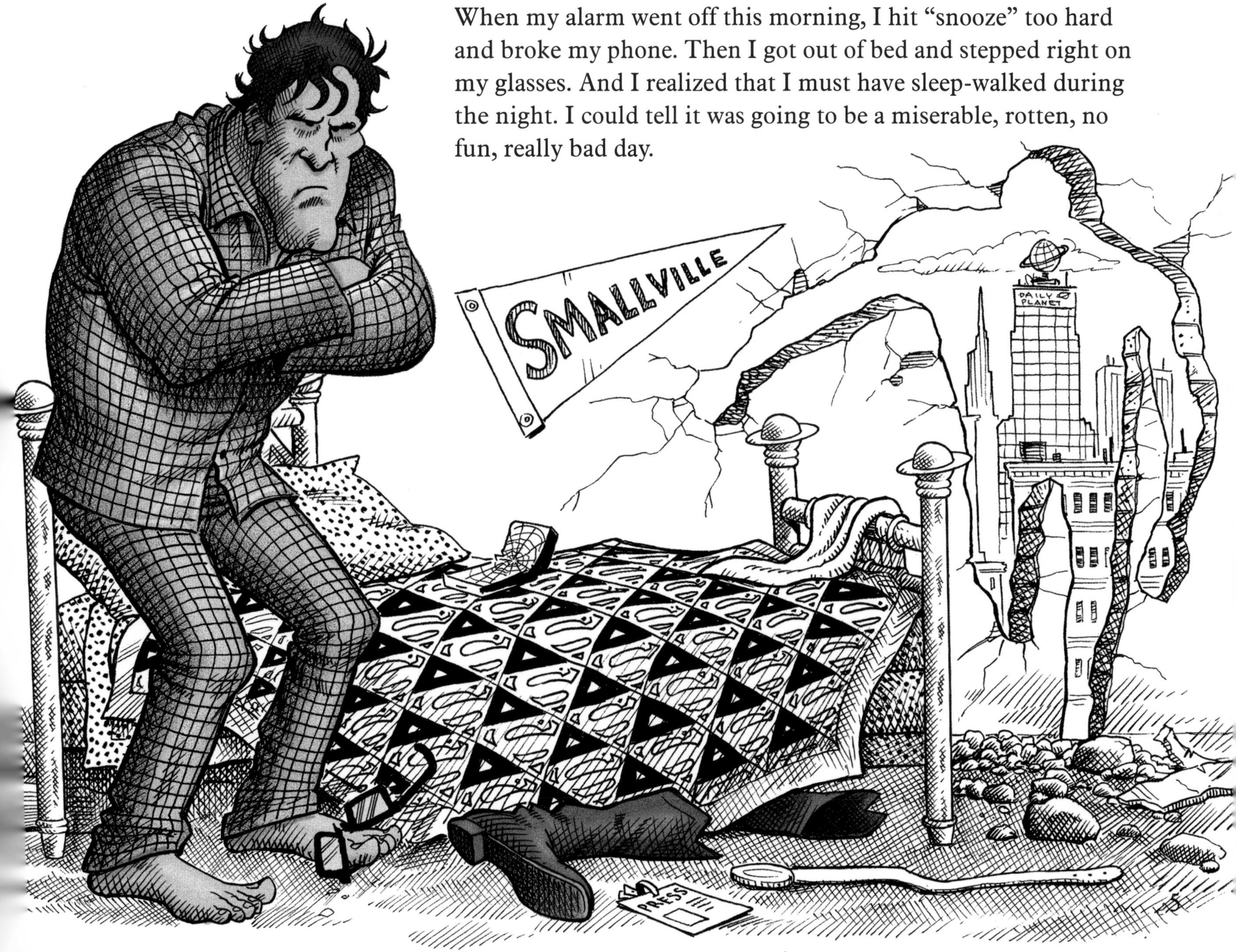
SMALLVILLE
DAILY PLANET
PRESS

Then while I was washing my face, I got soap in my eyes. And when I was rubbing my eyes, I accidentally used my heat vision and made the shampoo bottle explode.

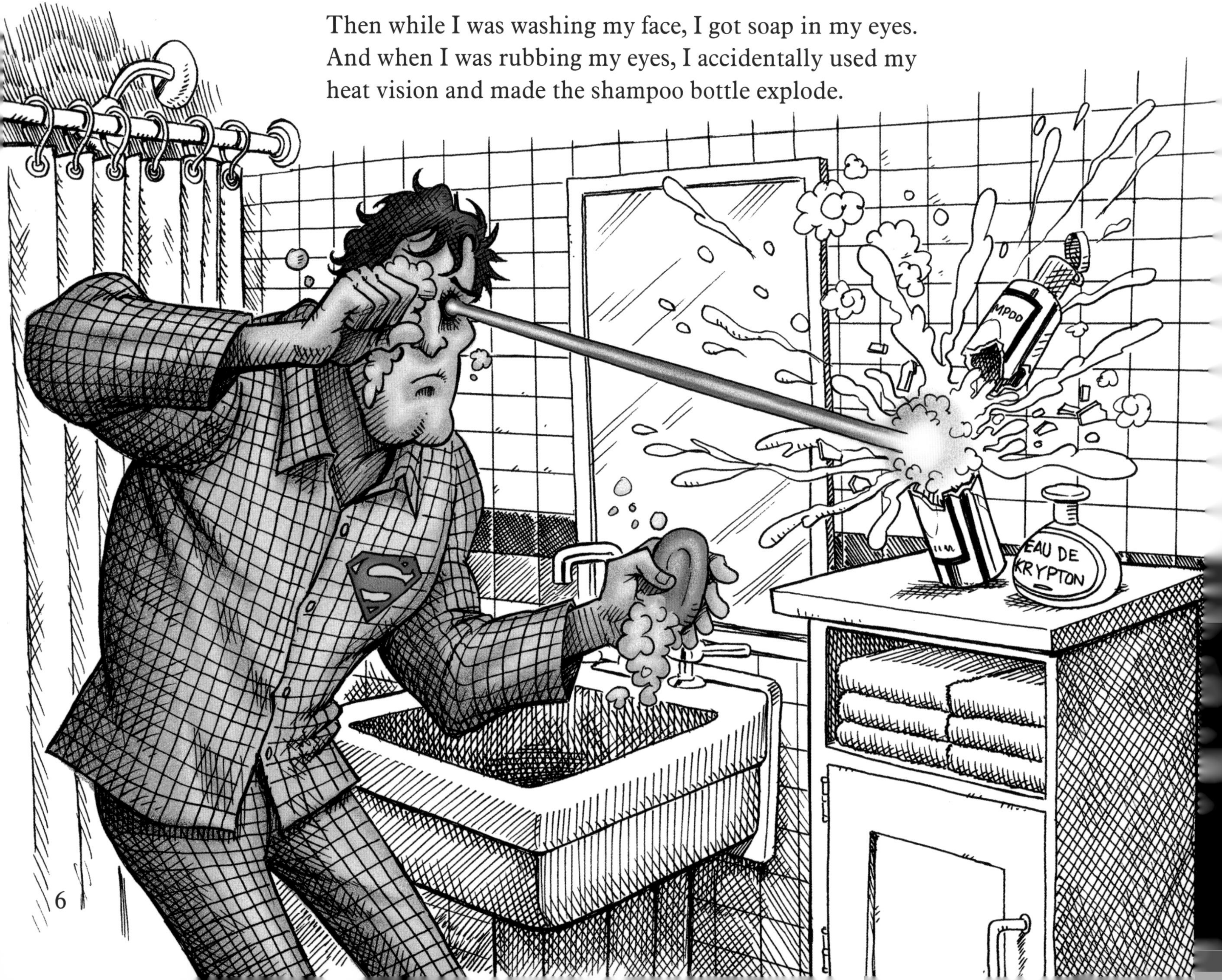
EAU DE
KRYPTON

I'm just going to move to the Fortress of Solitude.

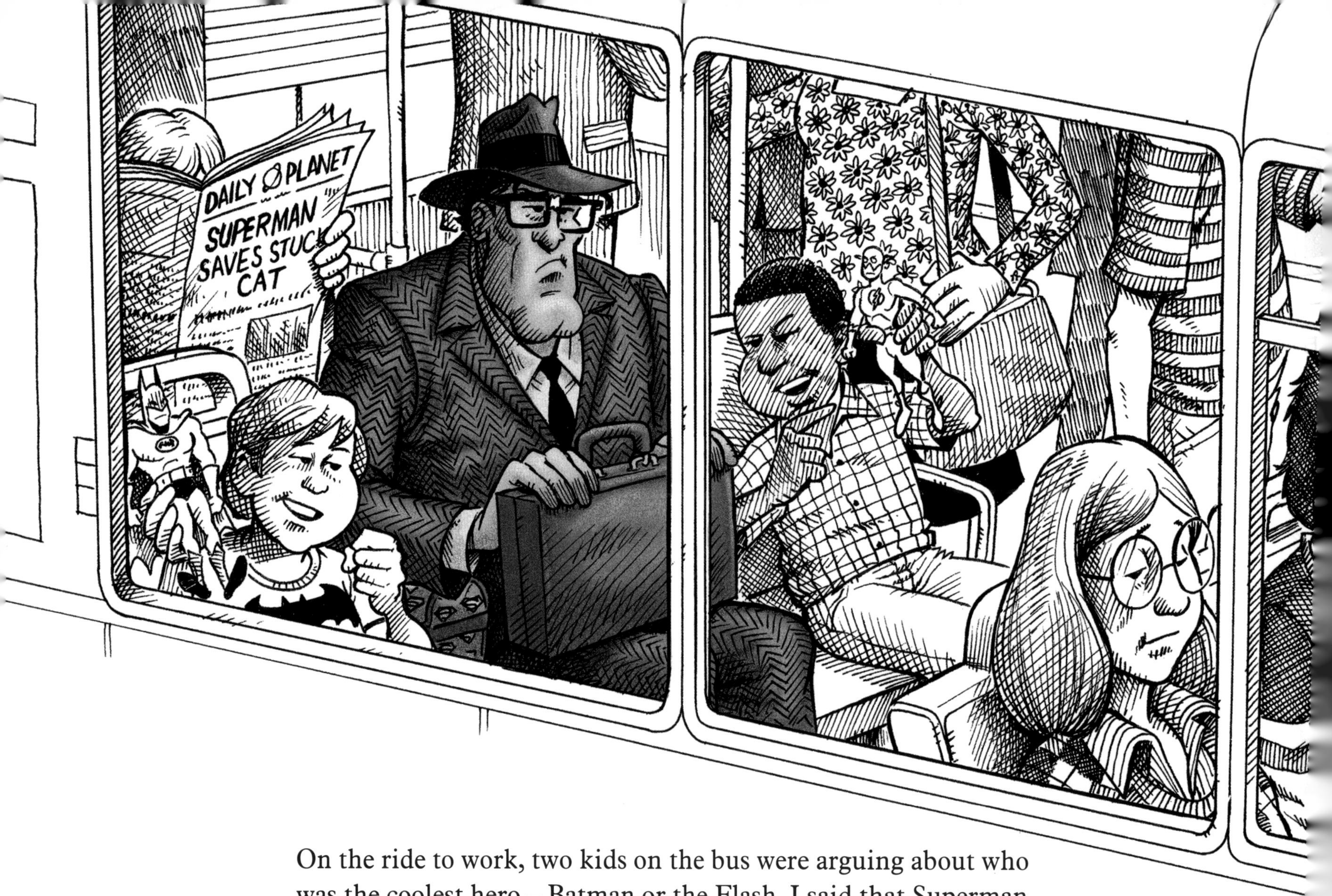
DAILY PLANET
SUPERMAN SAVES STUCK CAT

On the ride to work, two kids on the bus were arguing about who was the coolest hero – Batman or the Flash. I said that Superman was cool, too. I said he could fly. I said he had super-strength. I said Superman has saved the world a whole bunch of times. They said nothing.

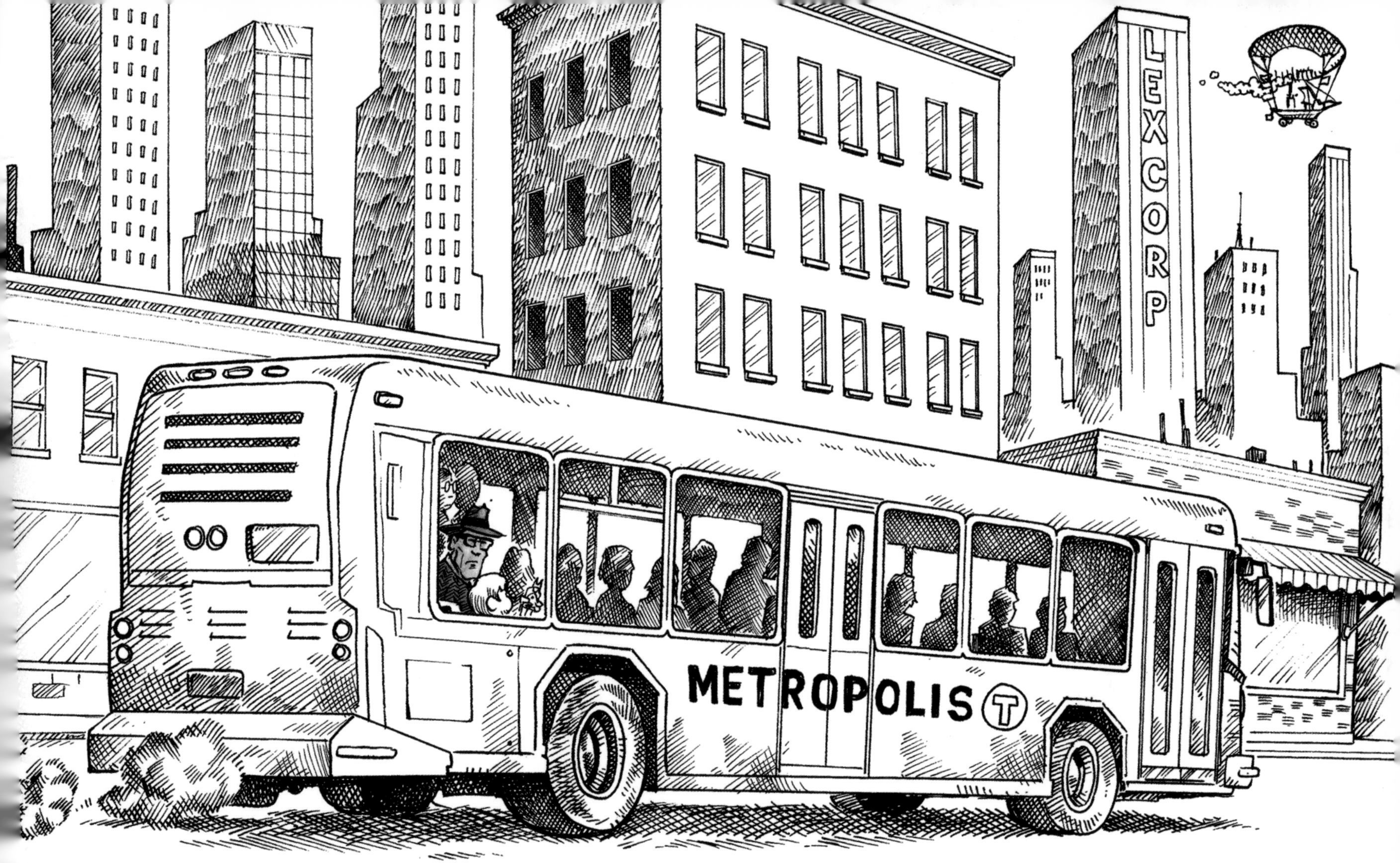
LEXCORP
METROPOLIS
T

I knew it was going to be a miserable, rotten, no fun, really bad day.

While I was still on the bus, Doomsday attacked the city and I had to rush off to fight him and I left my lunch on the bus.

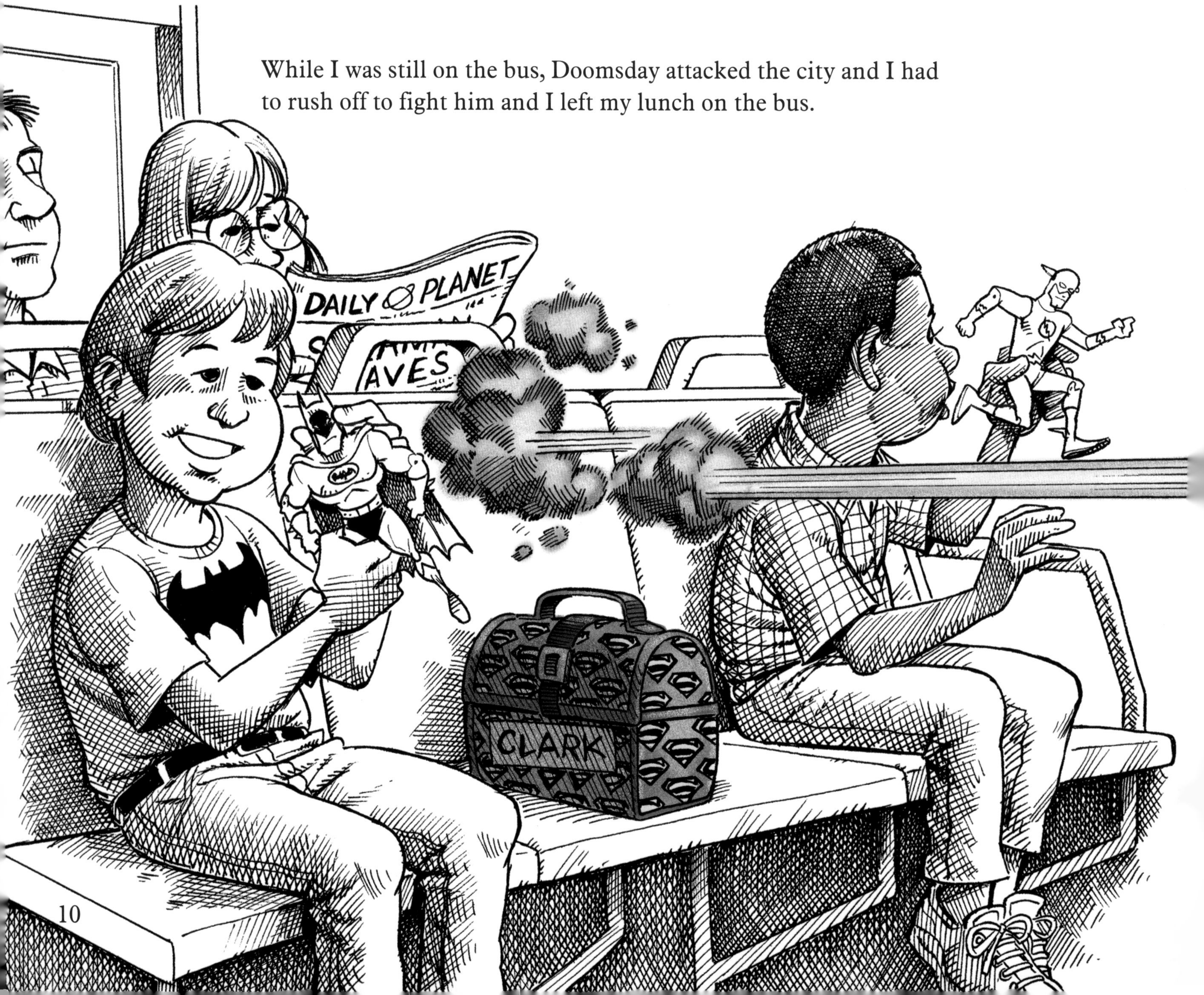
DAILY PLANET
AVES
CLARK

While I was changing, my new suit landed right in a puddle.
Then I realized my costume was on inside out.
I knew it was going to be a miserable, rotten, no fun, really bad day.

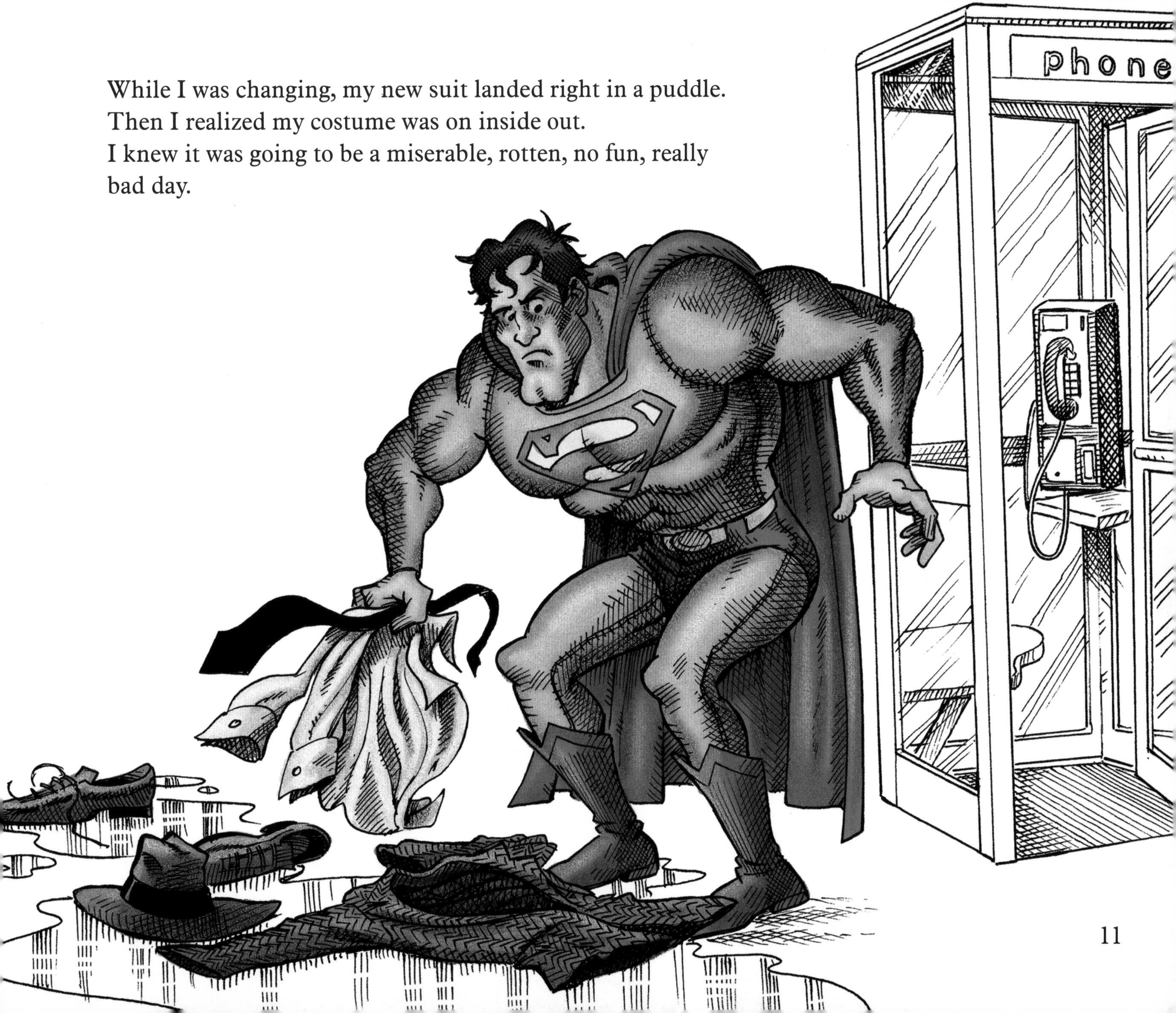
phone

I knew because after I beat Doomsday, one of those kids said, "Flash would've done it much faster." And the other kid said, "Batman would've looked cooler doing it."

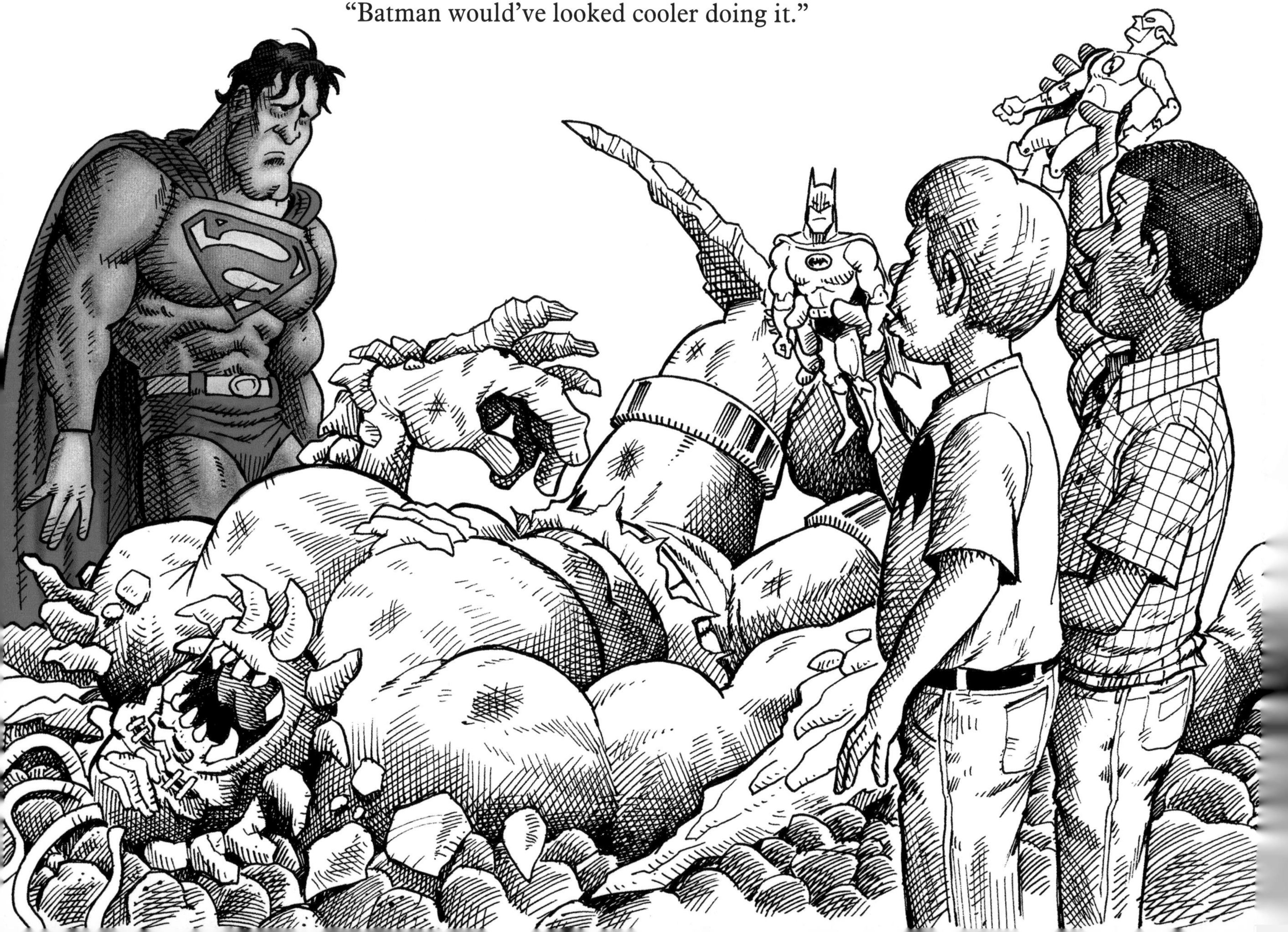

Then I was late for work and Perry yelled at me in front of everyone. And he said my suit was a mess. Who cares about a suit? I just saved Metropolis!

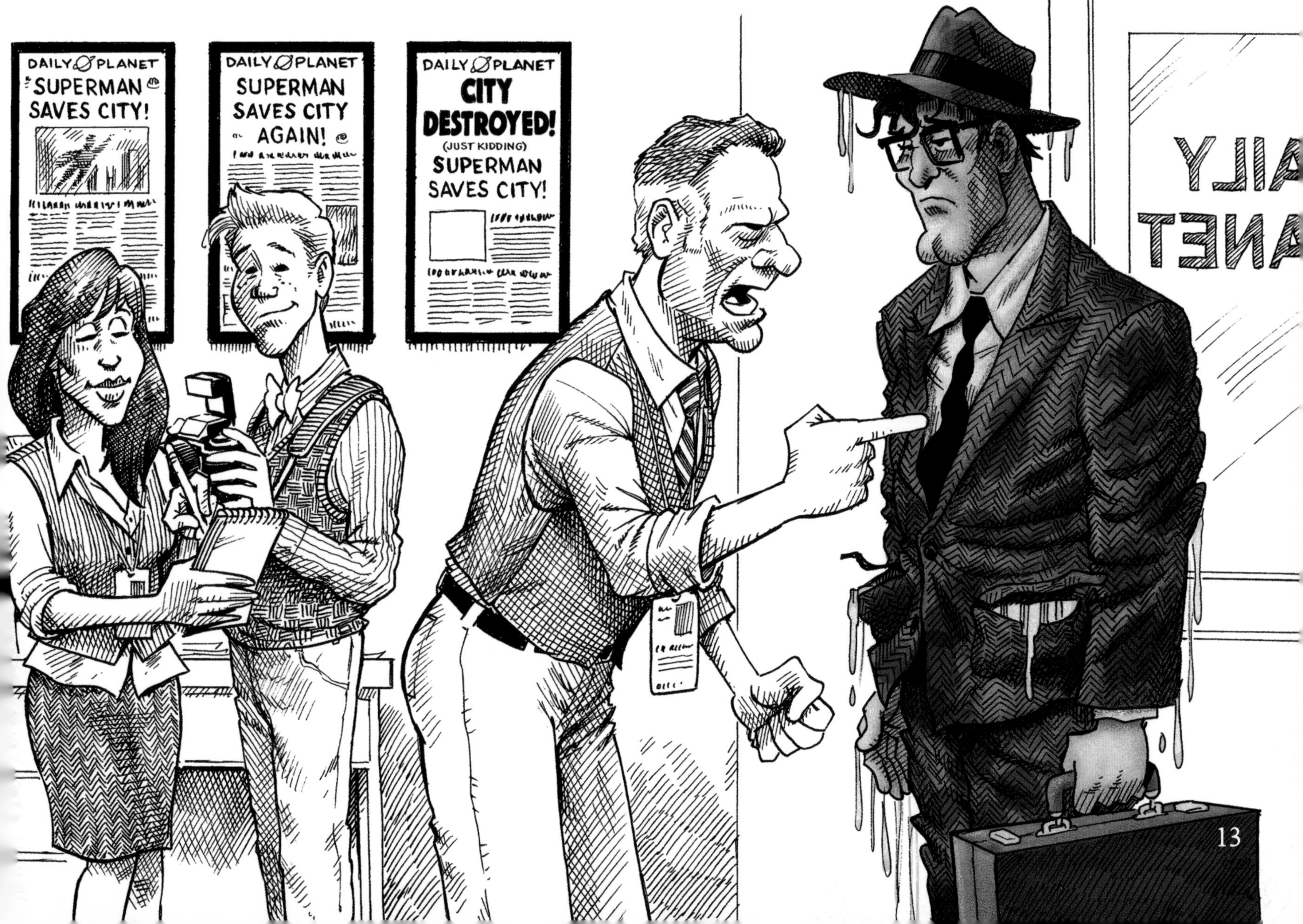
DAILY PLANET
SUPERMAN SAVES CITY!
DAILY PLANET
SUPERMAN SAVES CITY AGAIN!
DAILY PLANET
CITY DESTROYED!
(JUST KIDDING)
SUPERMAN SAVES CITY!

At work, Lois got to write about the President's visit.
And Jimmy got to take pictures of a motorcycle race.
Guess who had to cover a flower show?

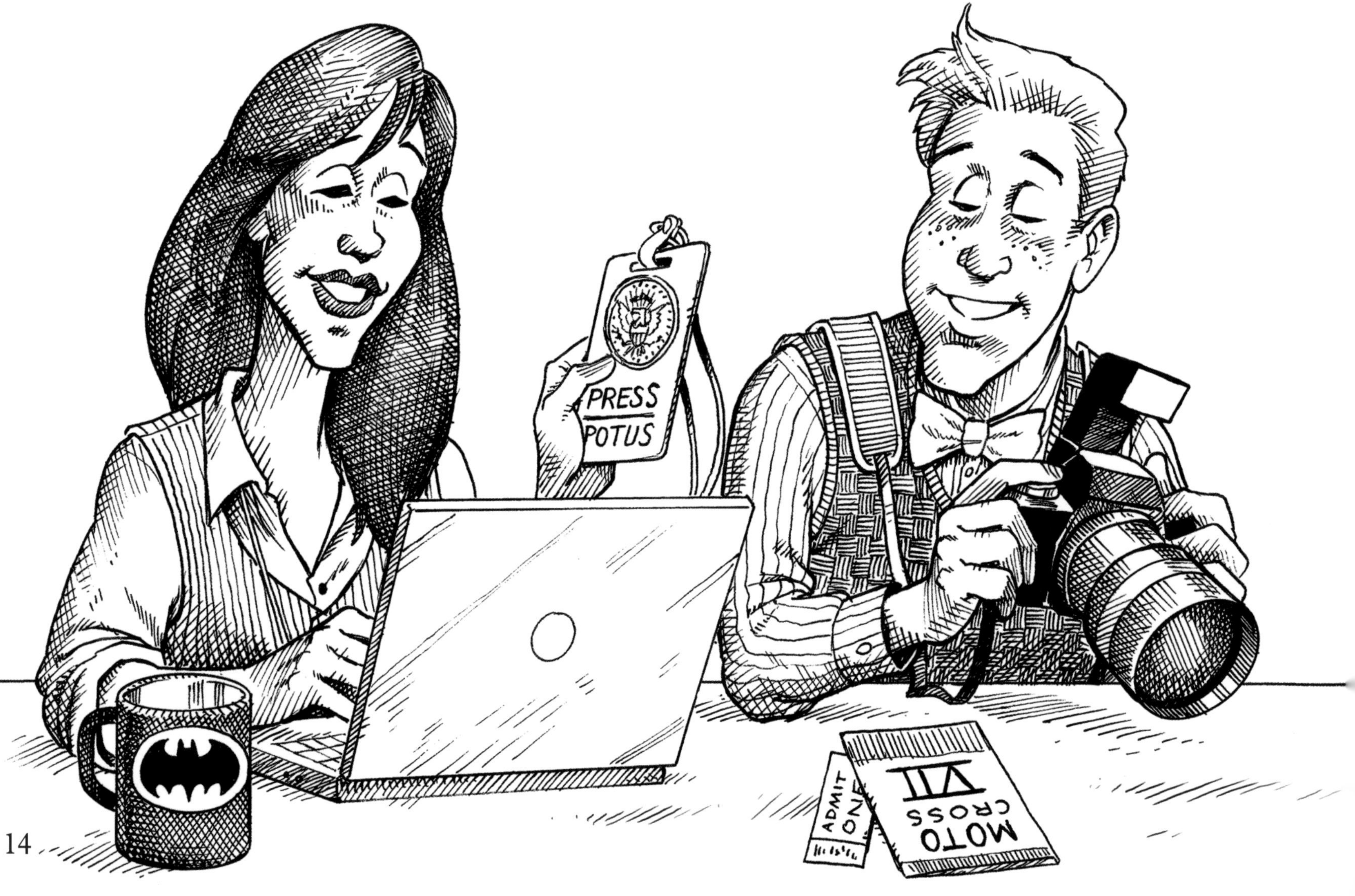

PRESS
POTUS
ADMIT ONE
MOTO CROSS VII

It was a miserable, rotten, no fun, really bad day.

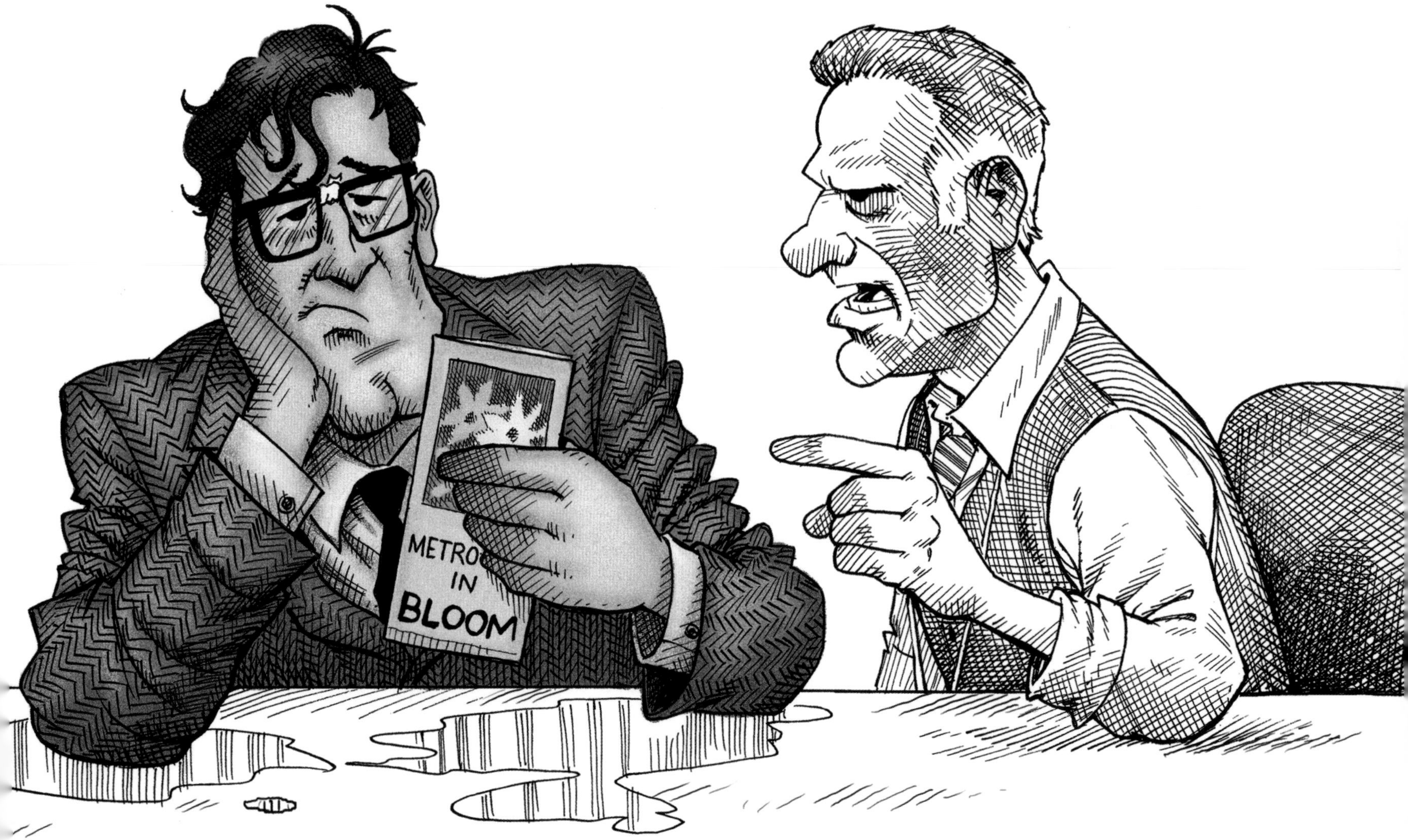
METRO
IN
BLOOM

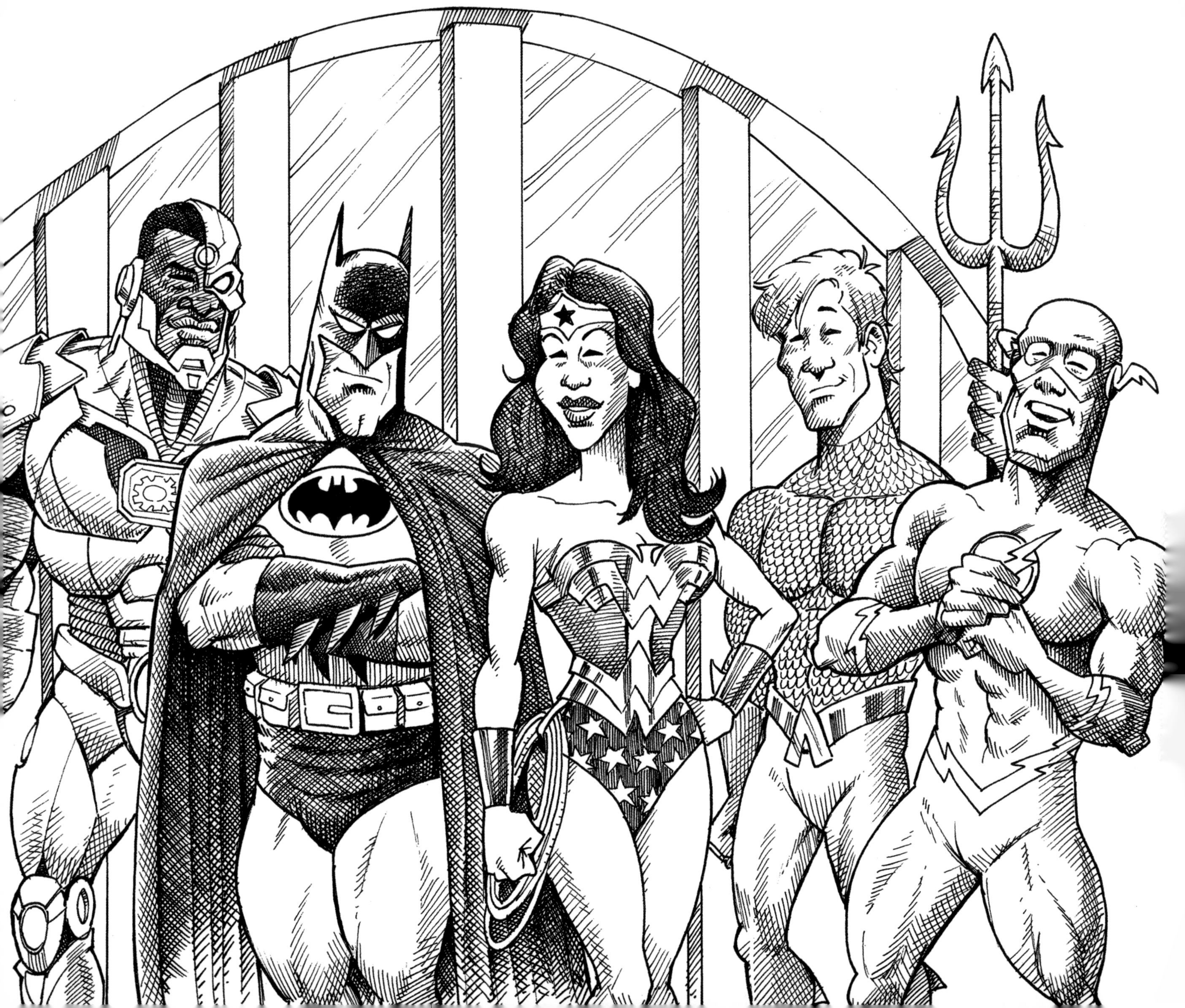

That's what it was, because after work, I was at the Hall of Justice with all the other superheroes and I got stuck doing boring monitor duty. Green Lantern said, "At least you don't have to do this again until next week!"

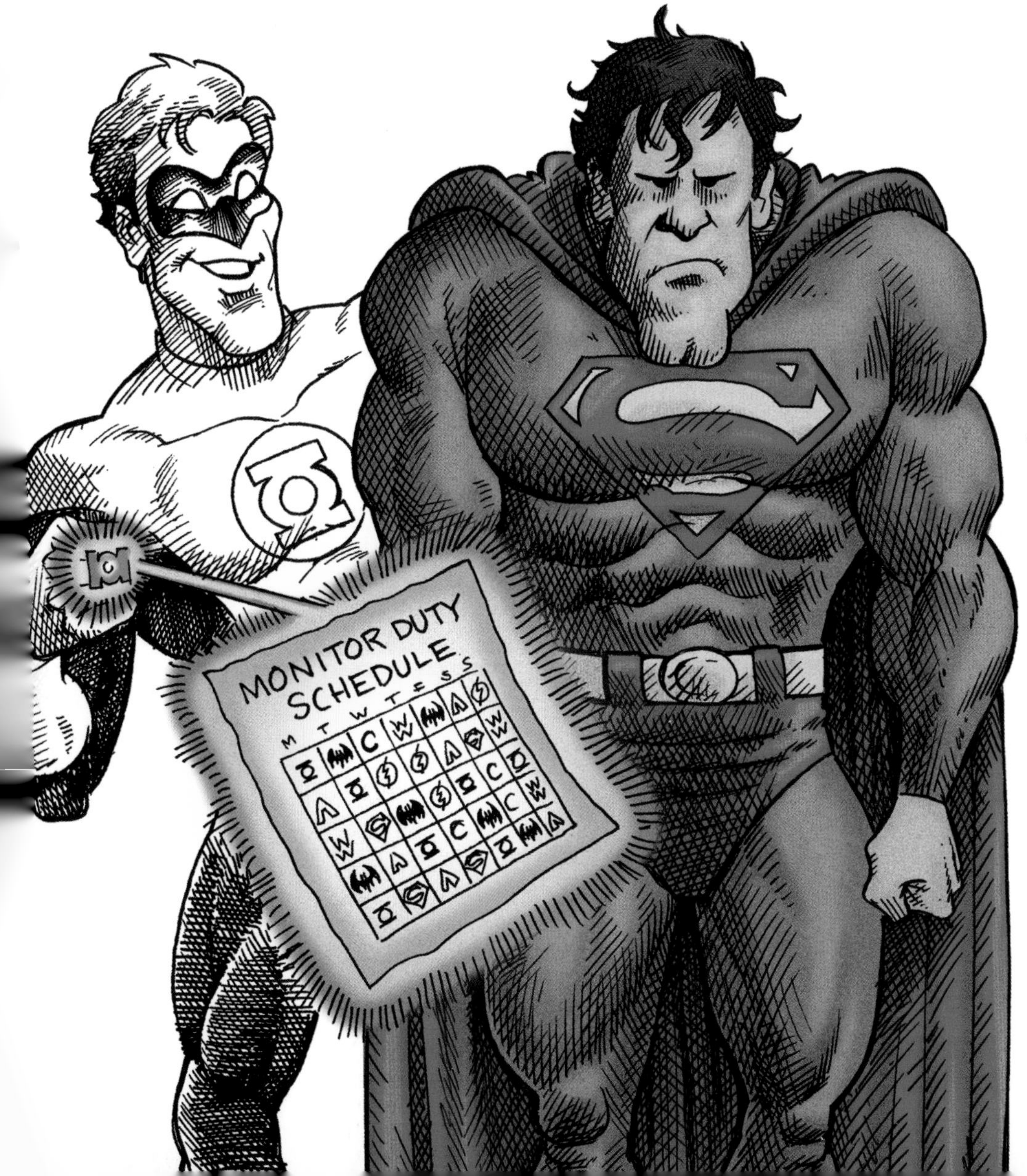
MONITOR DUTY
SCHEDULE

Next week, I said,
I'm moving to the Fortress of Solitude.

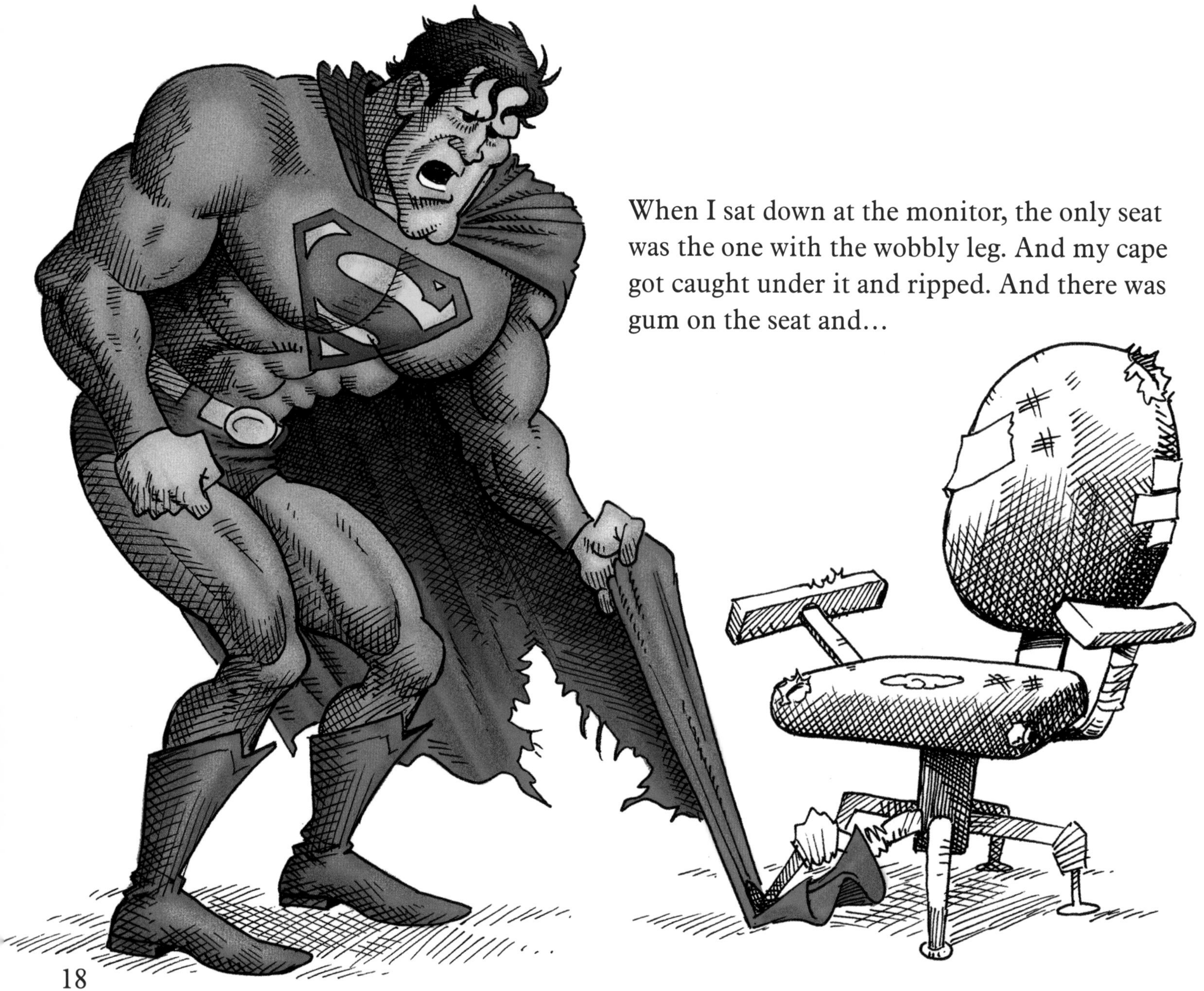

When I sat down at the monitor, the only seat was the one with the wobbly leg. And my cape got caught under it and ripped. And there was gum on the seat and...

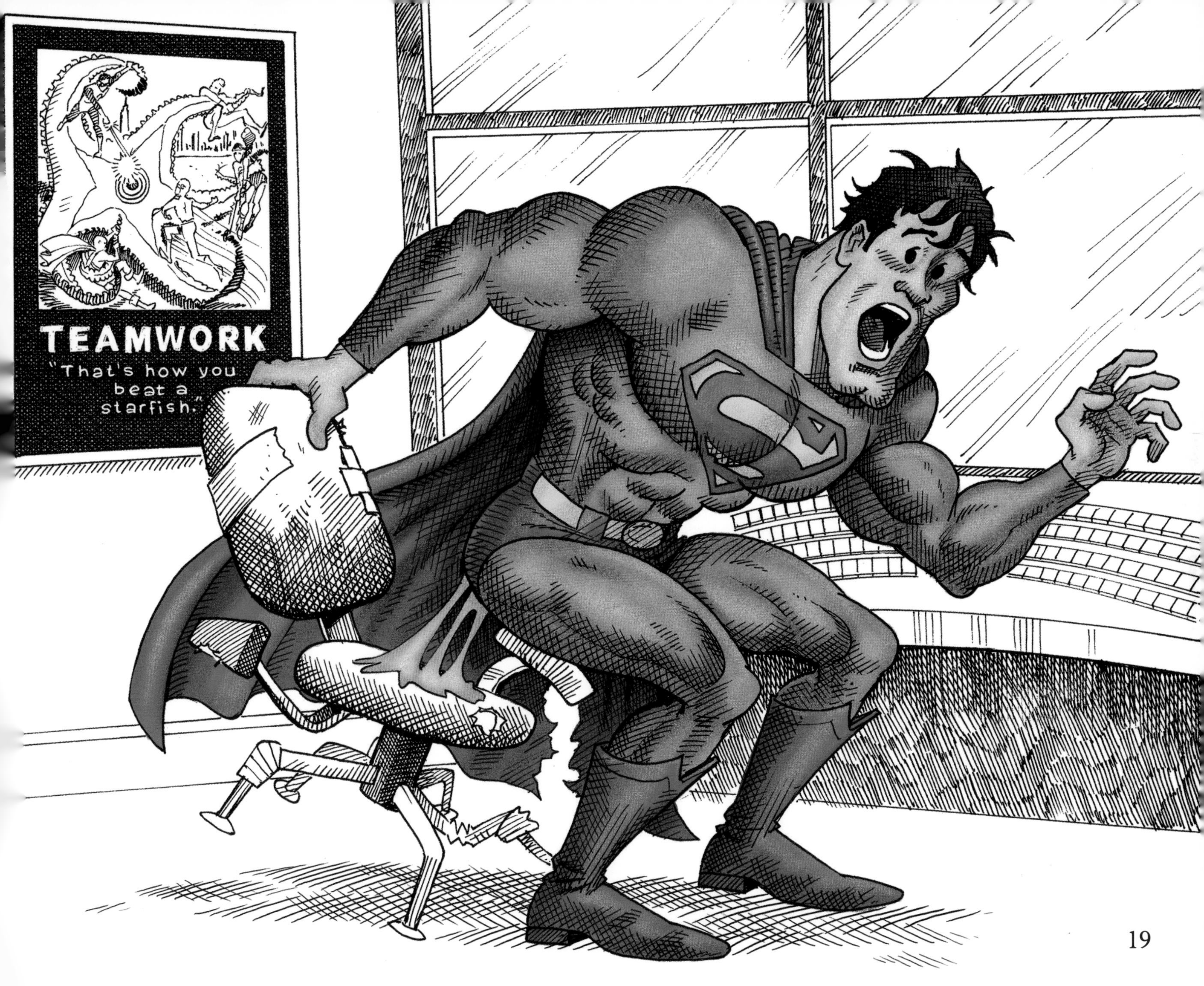
TEAMWORK
"That's how you beat a starfish."

...that was when a tour came by.

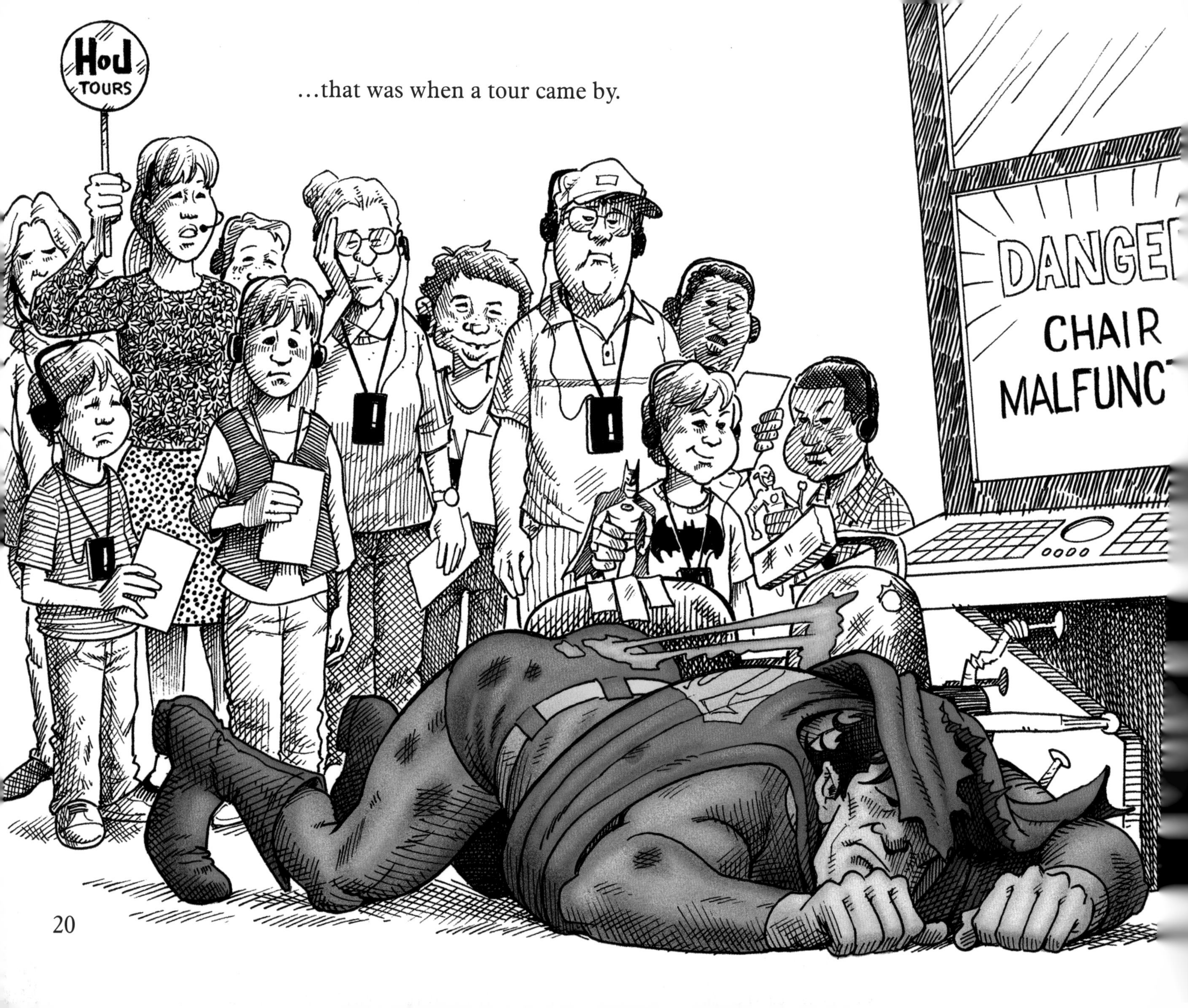
HoJ
TOURS
DANGE
CHAIR
MALFUNC

I am having a miserable, rotten, no fun, really bad day, I told everybody.
No one even looked at me.

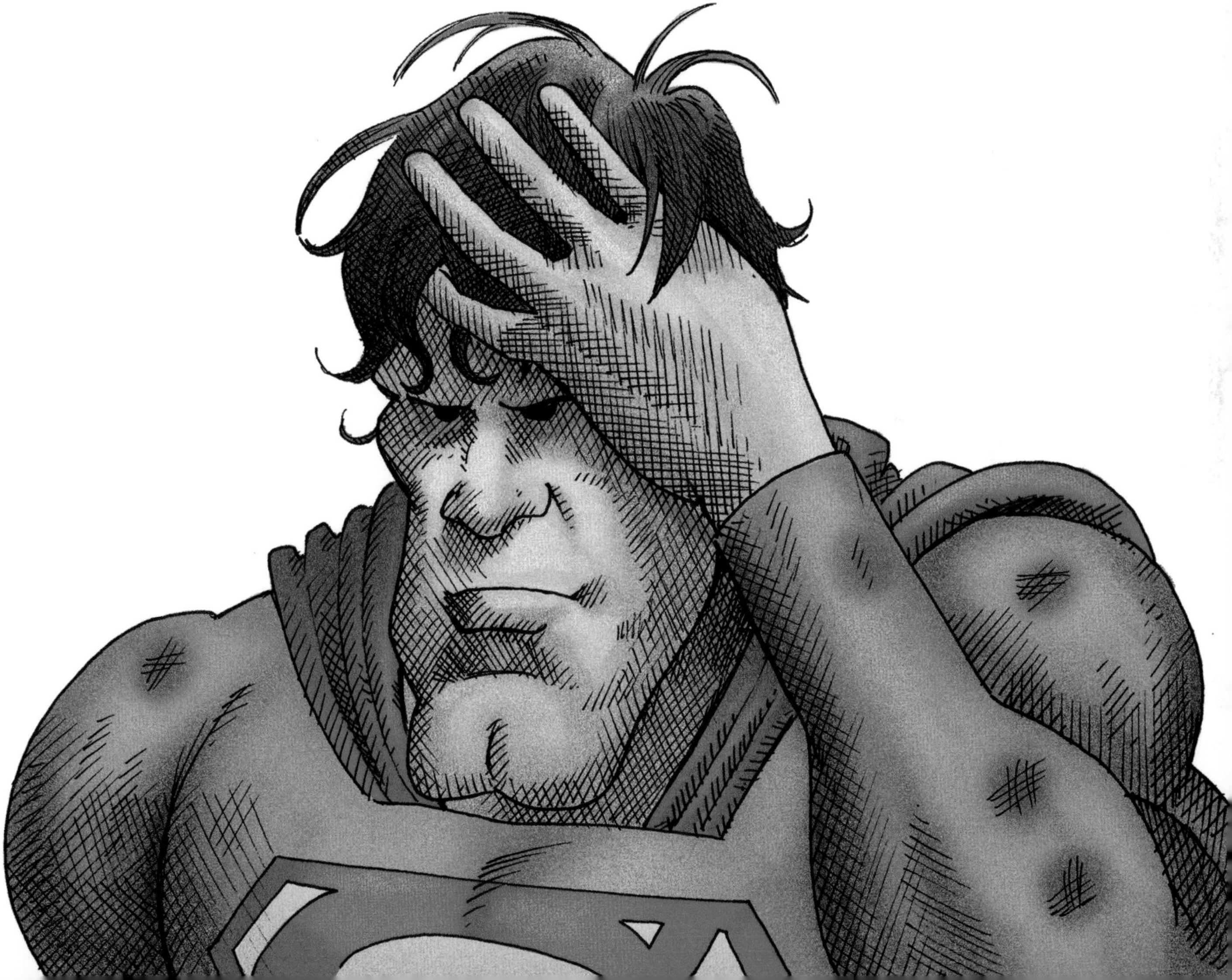

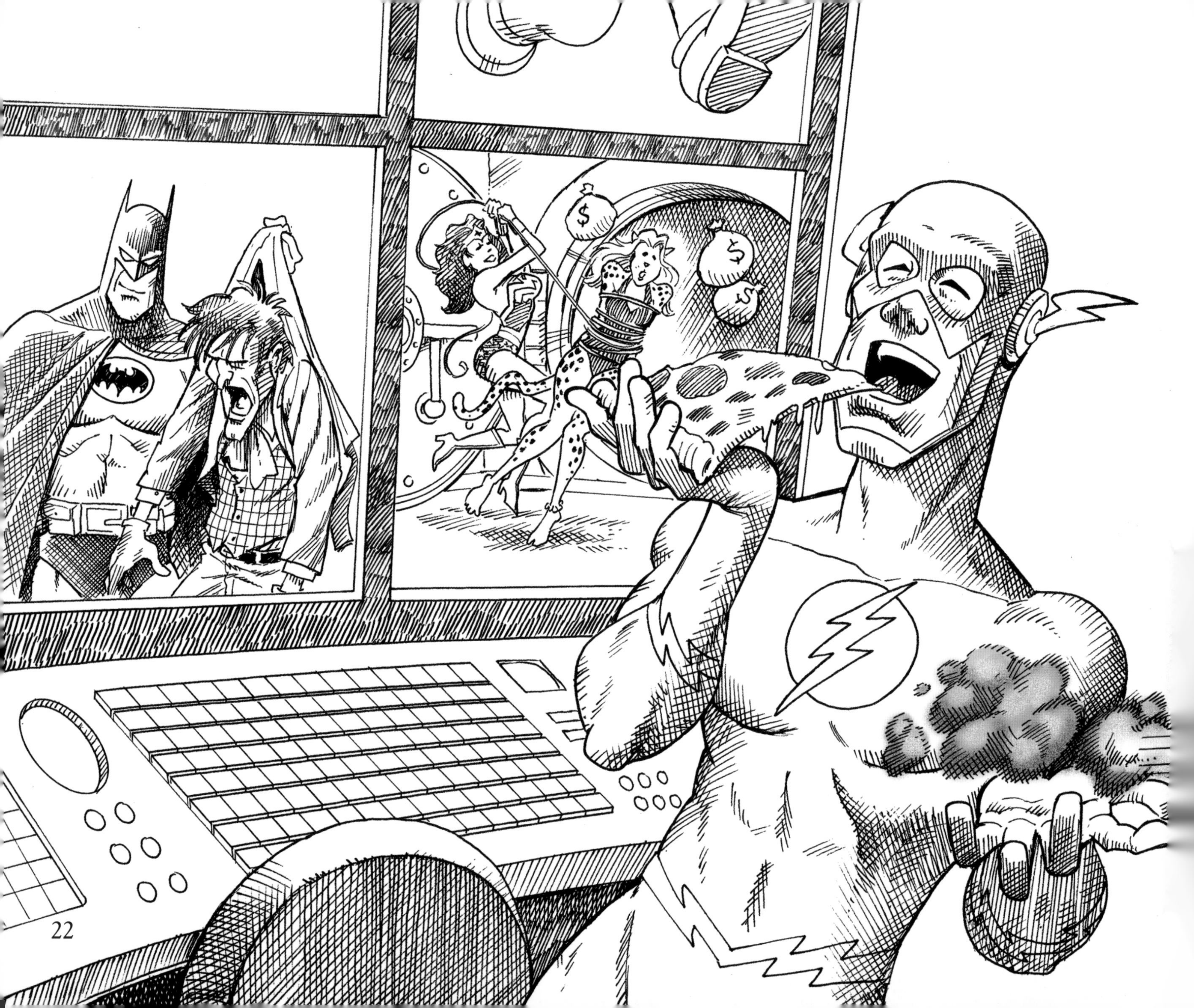

So, while I was stuck on monitor duty, Batman stopped the Joker from kidnapping the Mayor. Wonder Woman stopped Cheetah from robbing a bank. And I stopped the Flash from eating all the pizza. The only piece left had anchovies on it. I hate anchovies. They're the Kryptonite of pizza toppings.

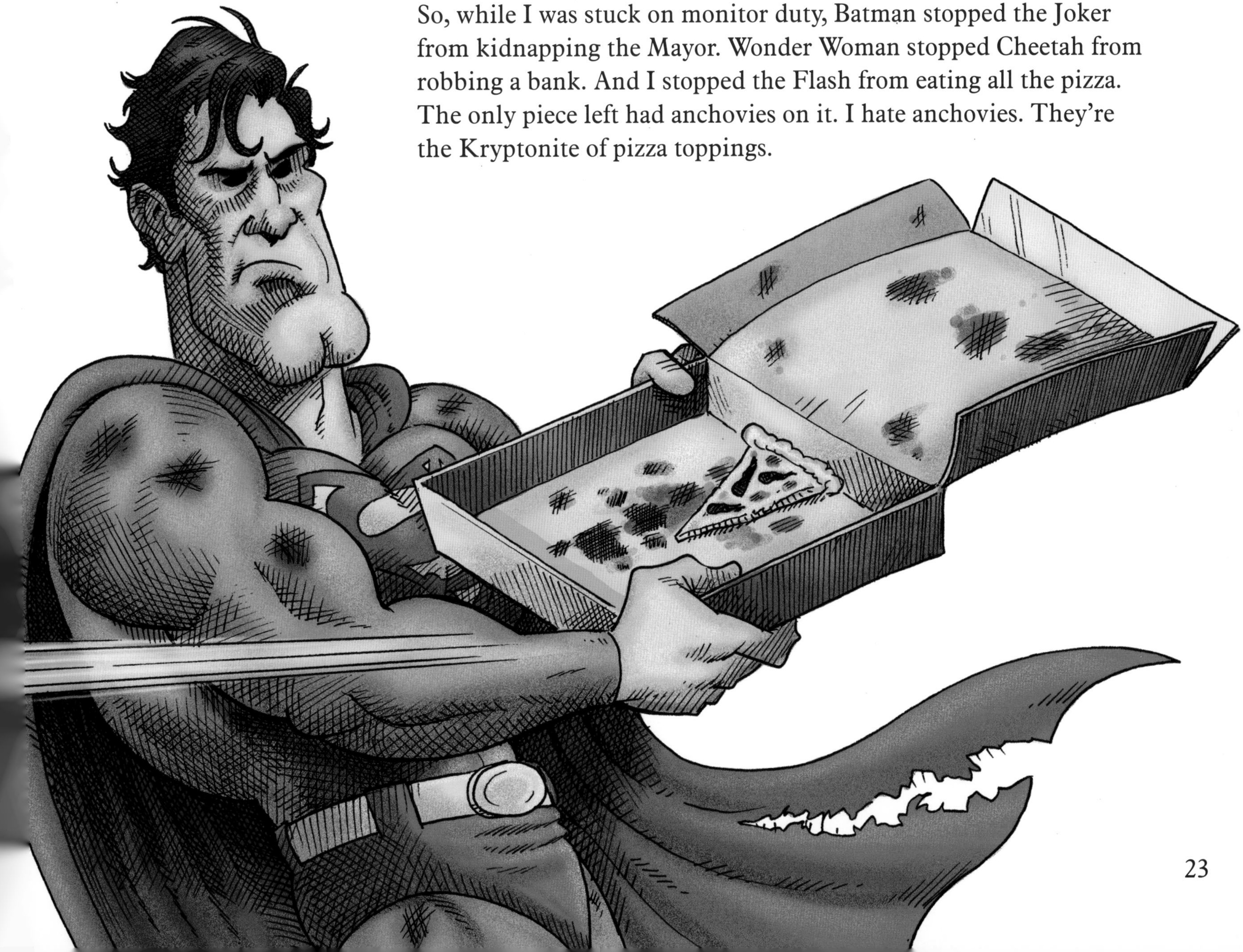

Batman got a key to the city. Wonder Woman got a parade in her honor. I got some stale old pretzels from the vending machine. And the machine didn't give me my change back.

It was a miserable, rotten, no fun, really bad day.

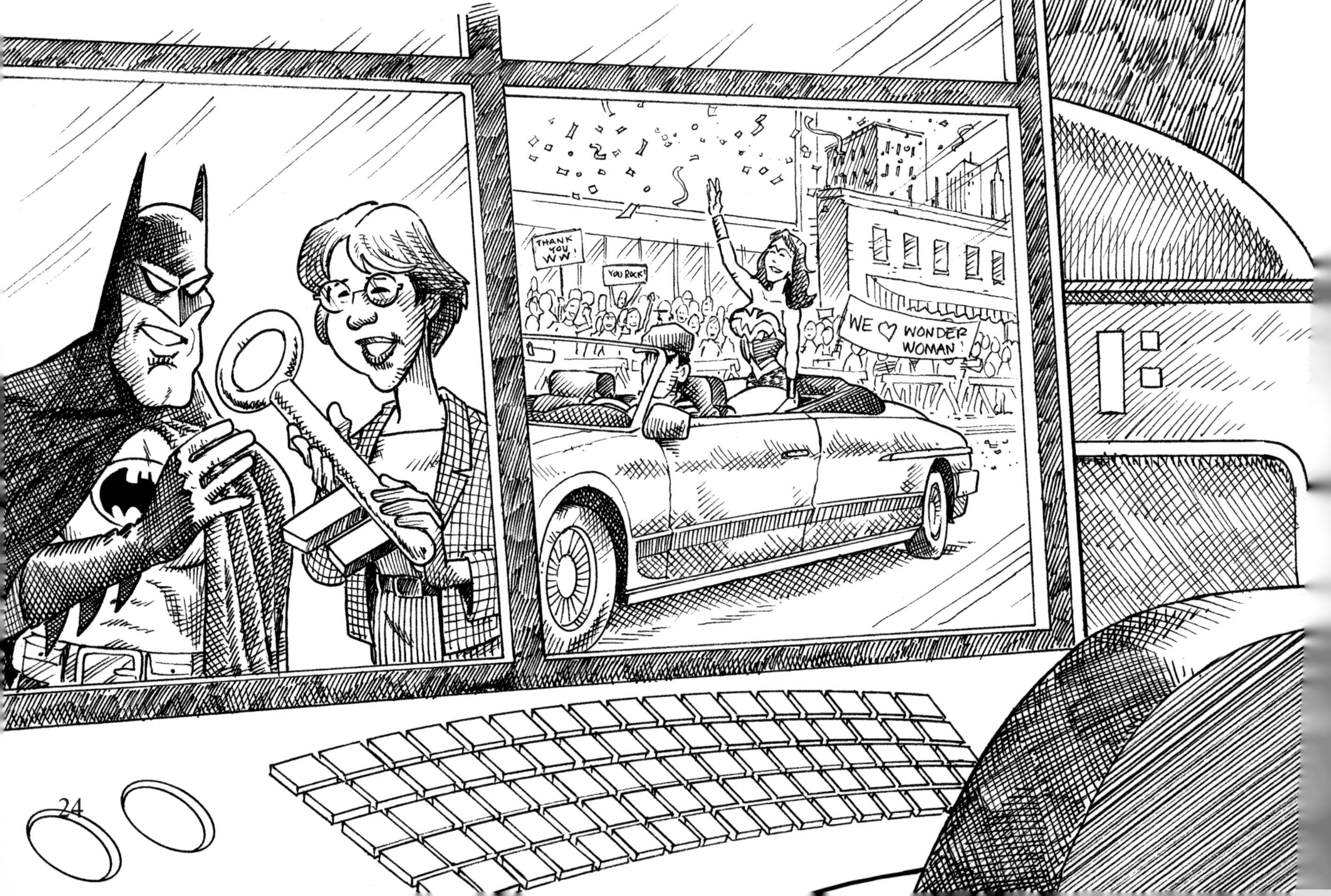
THANK YOU WW!
YOU ROCK!
WE ♡ WONDER WOMAN

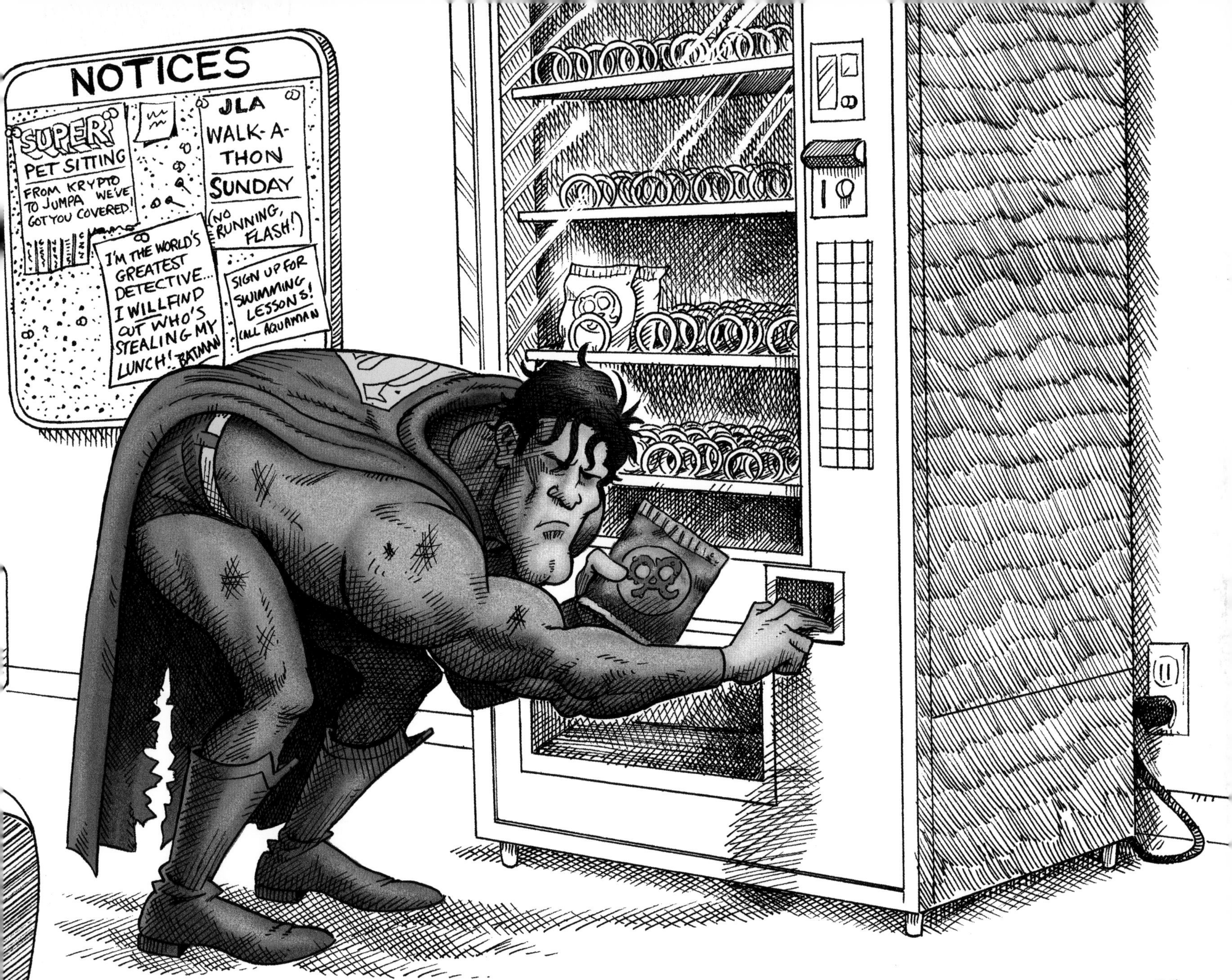
NOTICES
SUPER! PET SITTING
FROM KRYPTO TO JUMPA WE'VE GOT YOU COVERED!
JLA WALK-A-THON SUNDAY
(NO RUNNING, FLASH!)
I'M THE WORLD'S GREATEST DETECTIVE... I WILL FIND OUT WHO'S STEALING MY LUNCH! BATMAN
SIGN UP FOR SWIMMING LESSONS! CALL AQUAMAN

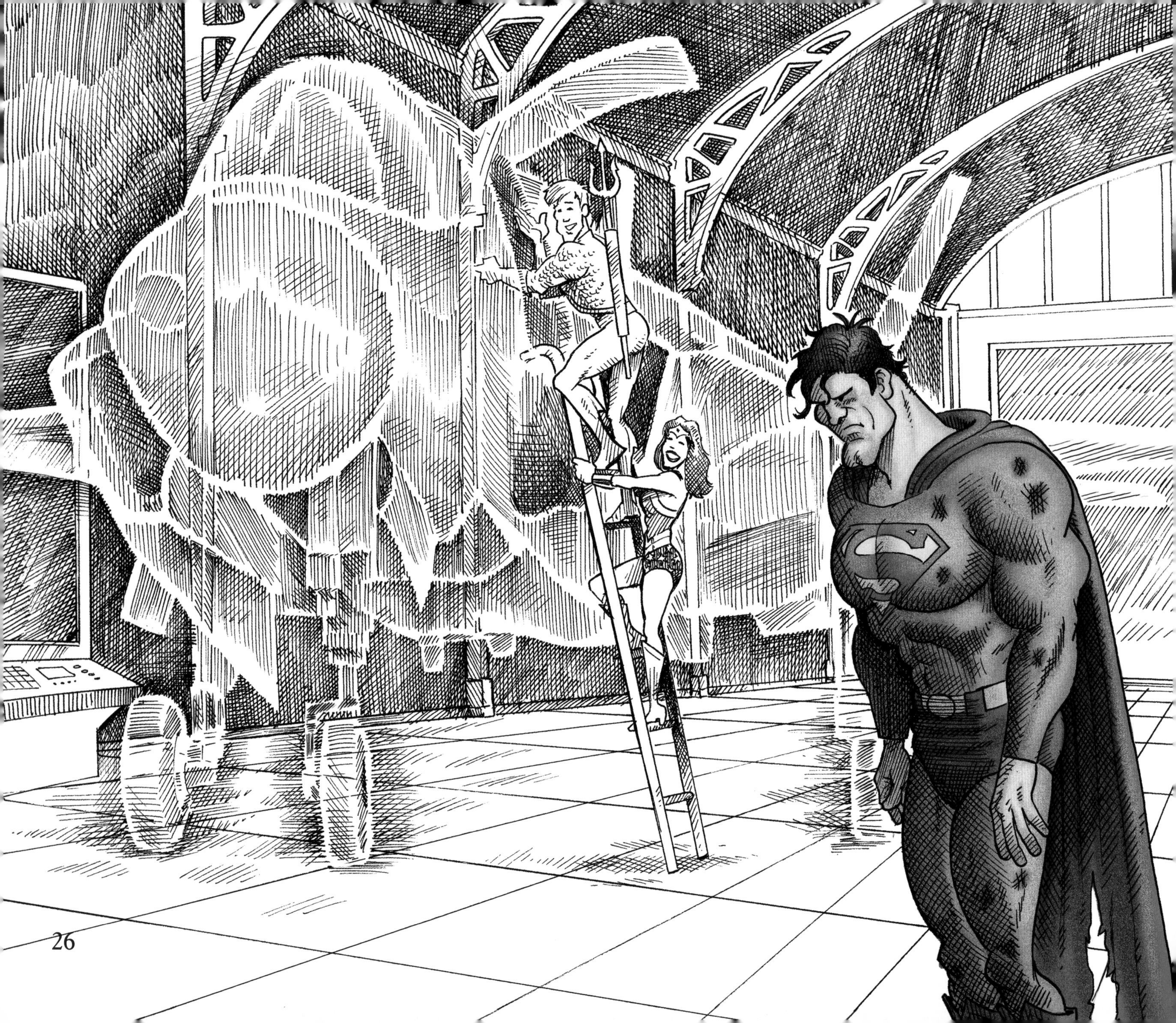

When it was time to leave the Hall of Justice, Wonder Woman gave Aquaman a ride home, even though I asked her first. She said I didn't need a ride, since I can fly. So what? I want to ride in an invisible jet!

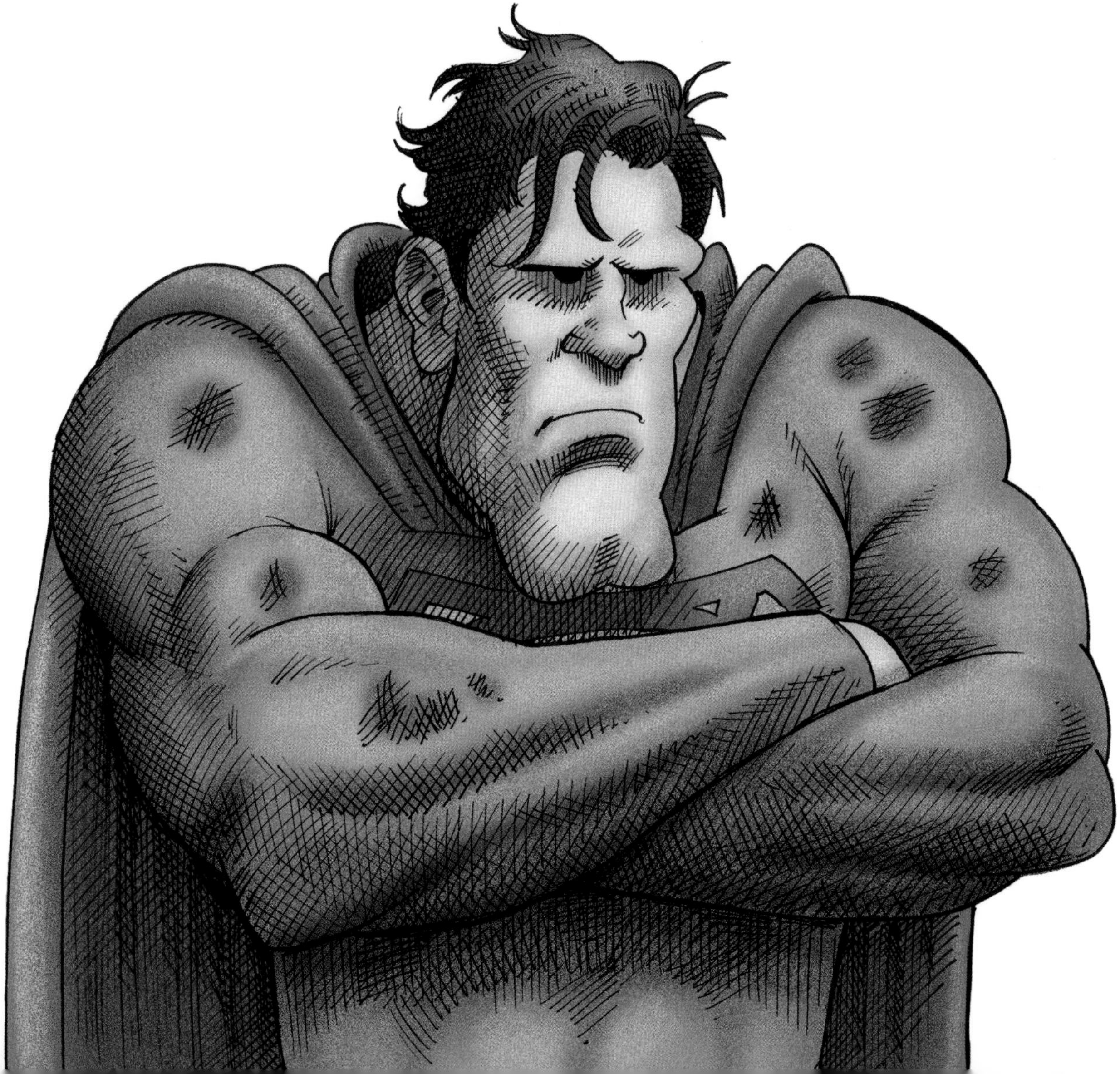

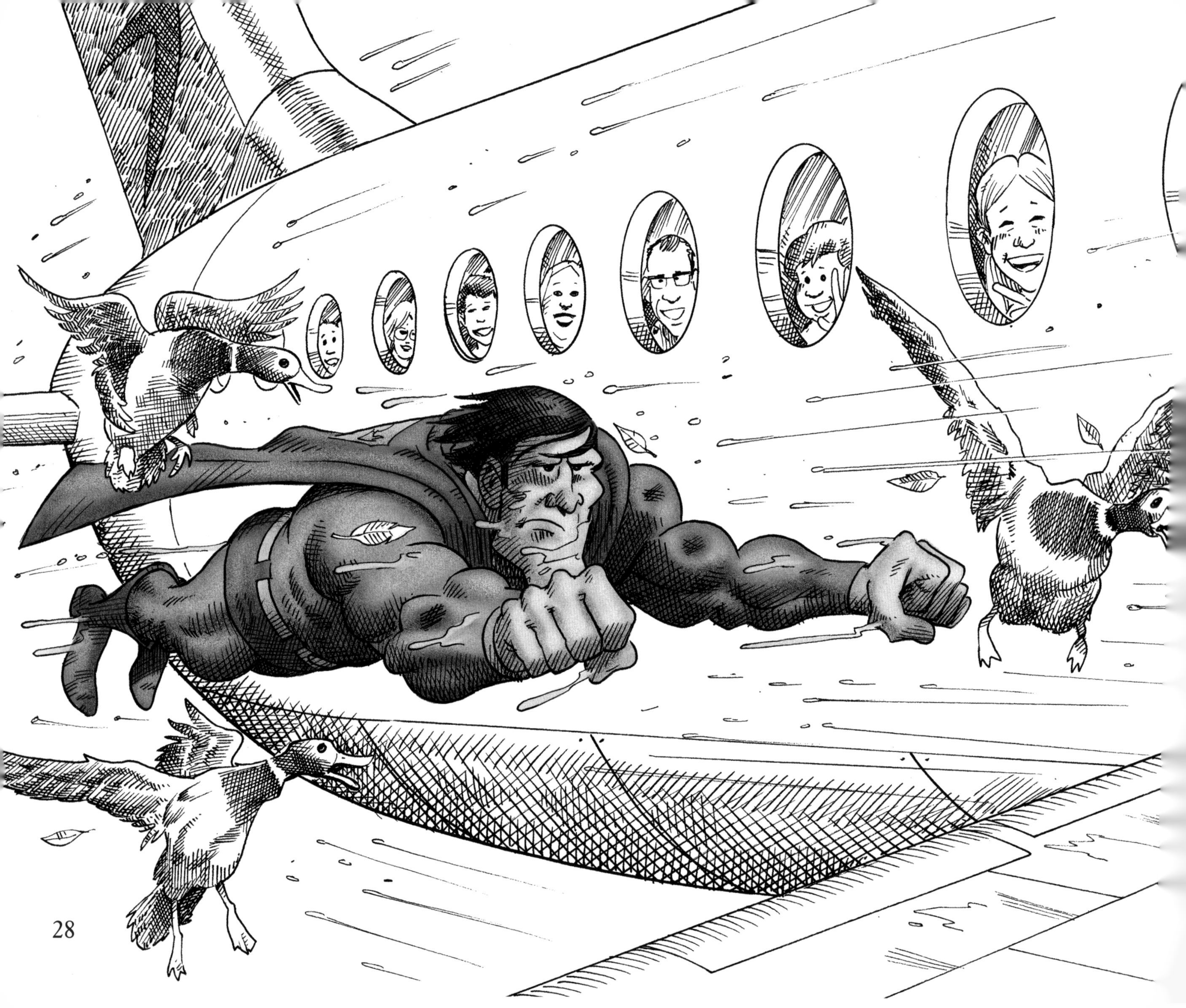

When I flew home, I got stuck behind a flock of ducks, and it started hailing, and a plane passed me and everyone laughed at me.

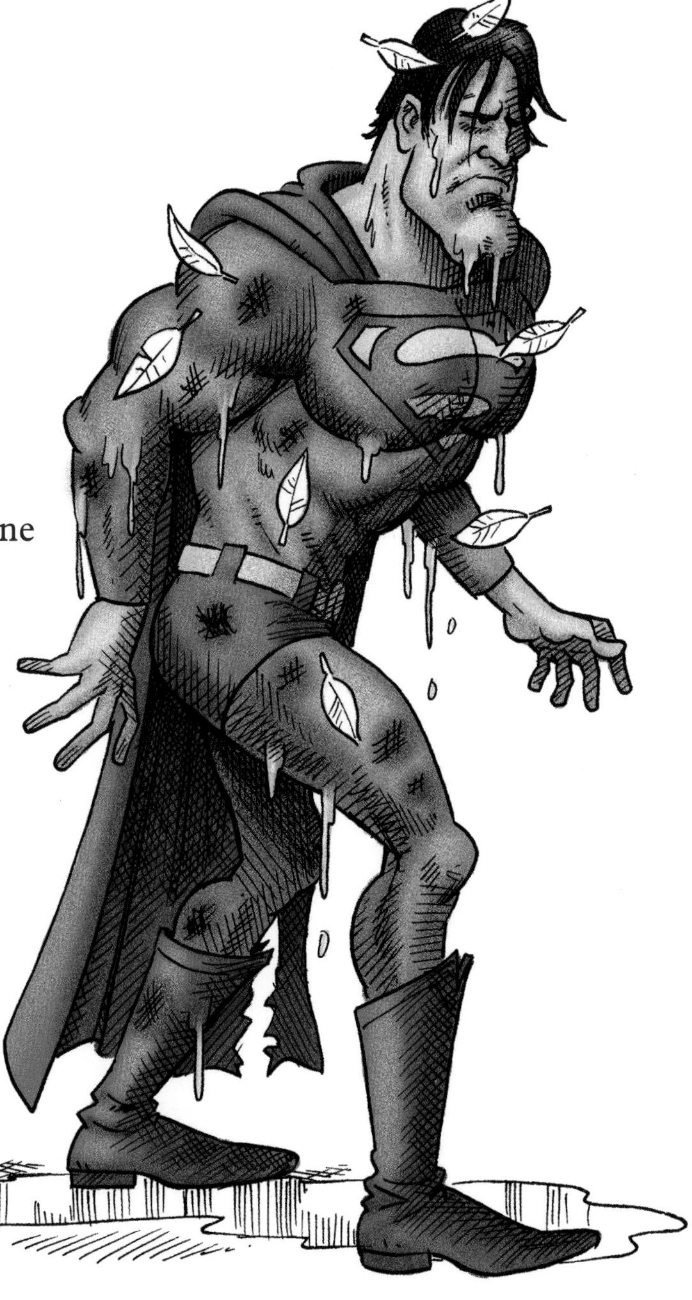

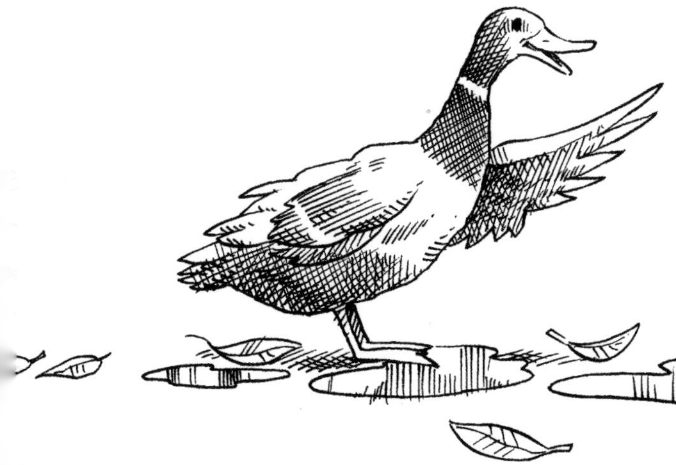

When I got back to my apartment, Ma messaged me, and I told her that the news said Lex Luthor found a giant chunk of Kryptonite. And General Zod escaped the Phantom Zone. And Lois was seen on a date with Bruce Wayne.

It has been a miserable, rotten, no fun, really bad day.

Ma says some days are like that.

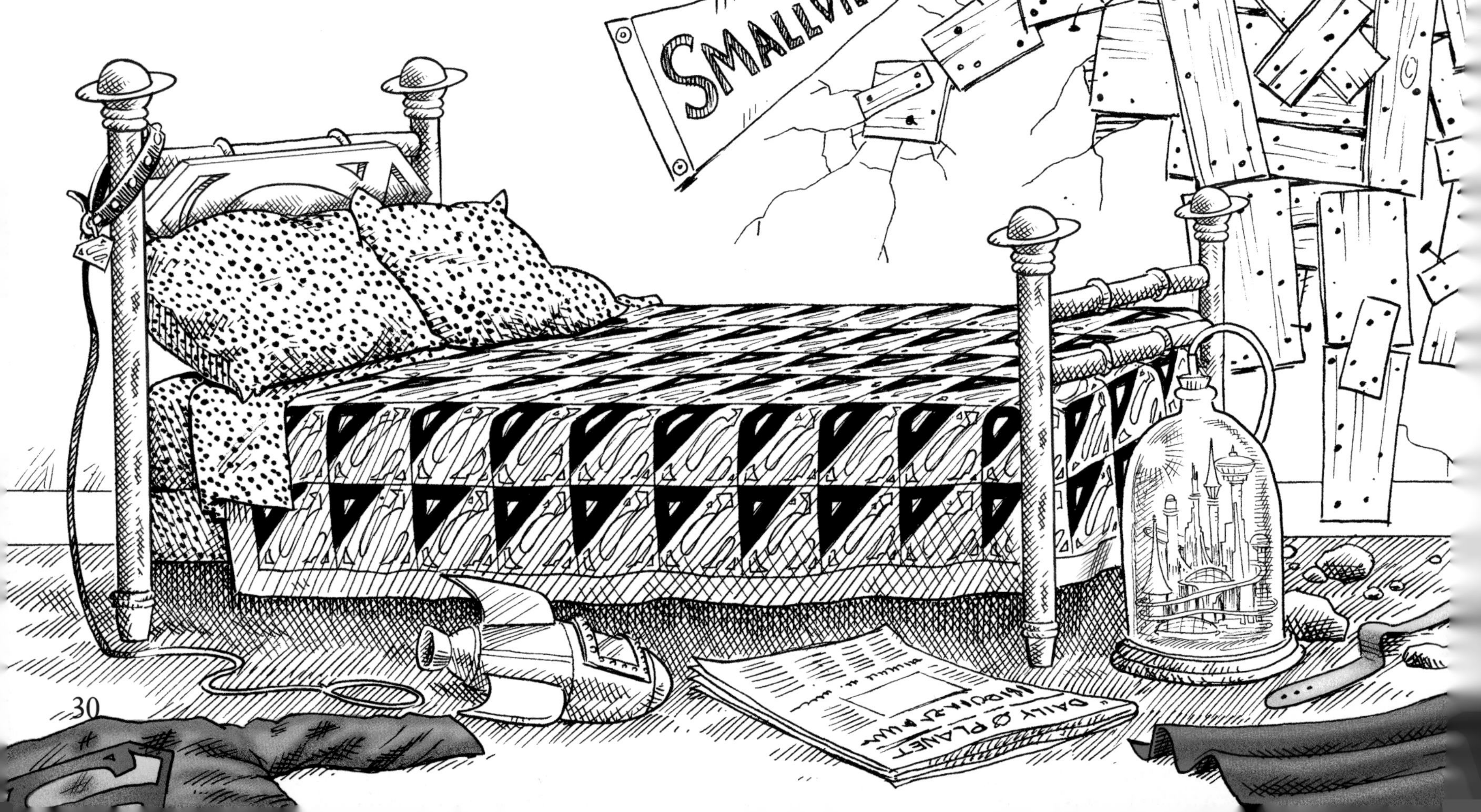
SMALLVILLE
DAILY PLANET

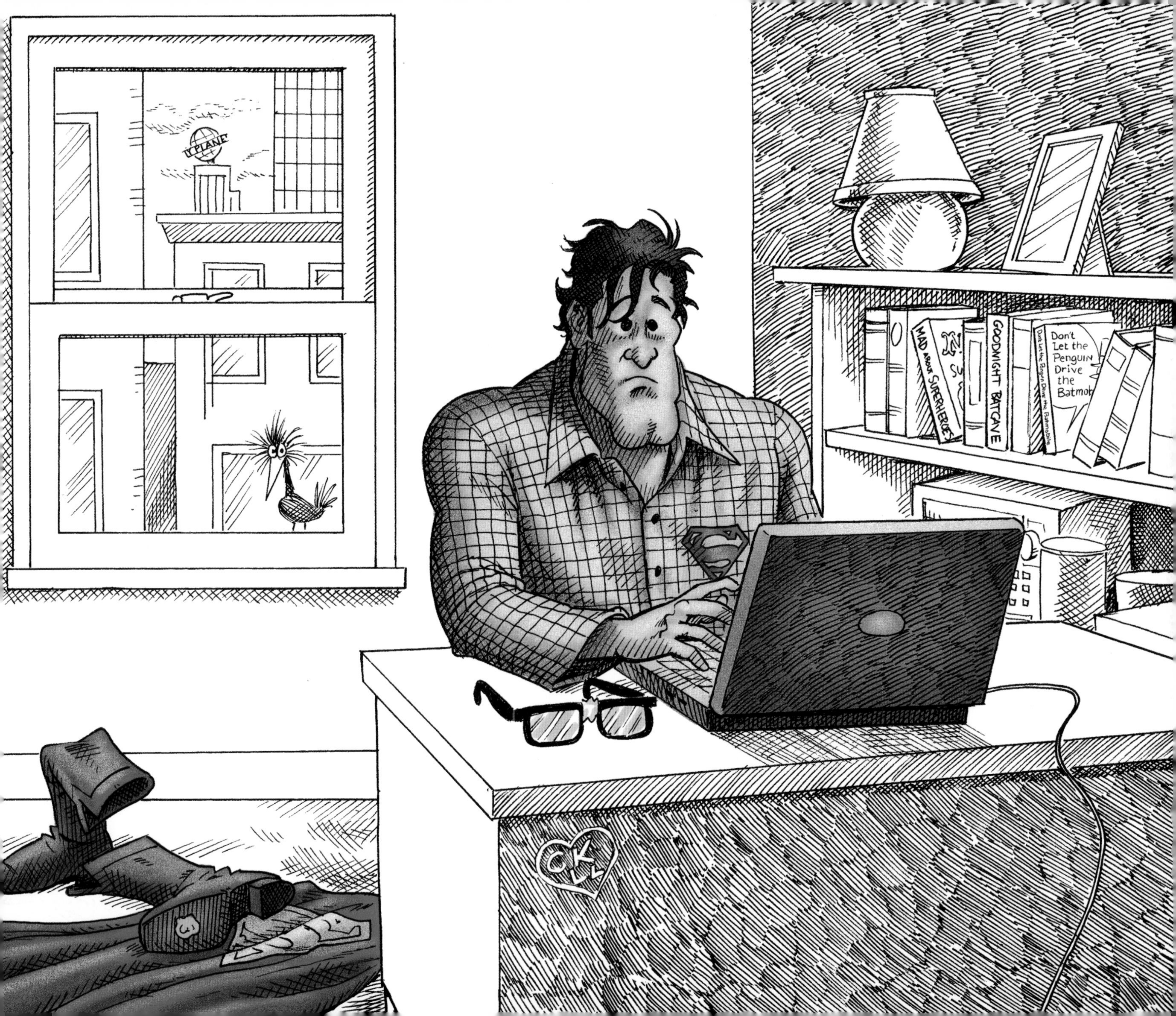

MAD ABOUT SUPERHEROES
GOODNIGHT BATCAVE
Don't Let the Penguin Drive the Batmobile
Don't Let the Penguin Drive the Batmob

Even in the Fortress of Solitude.

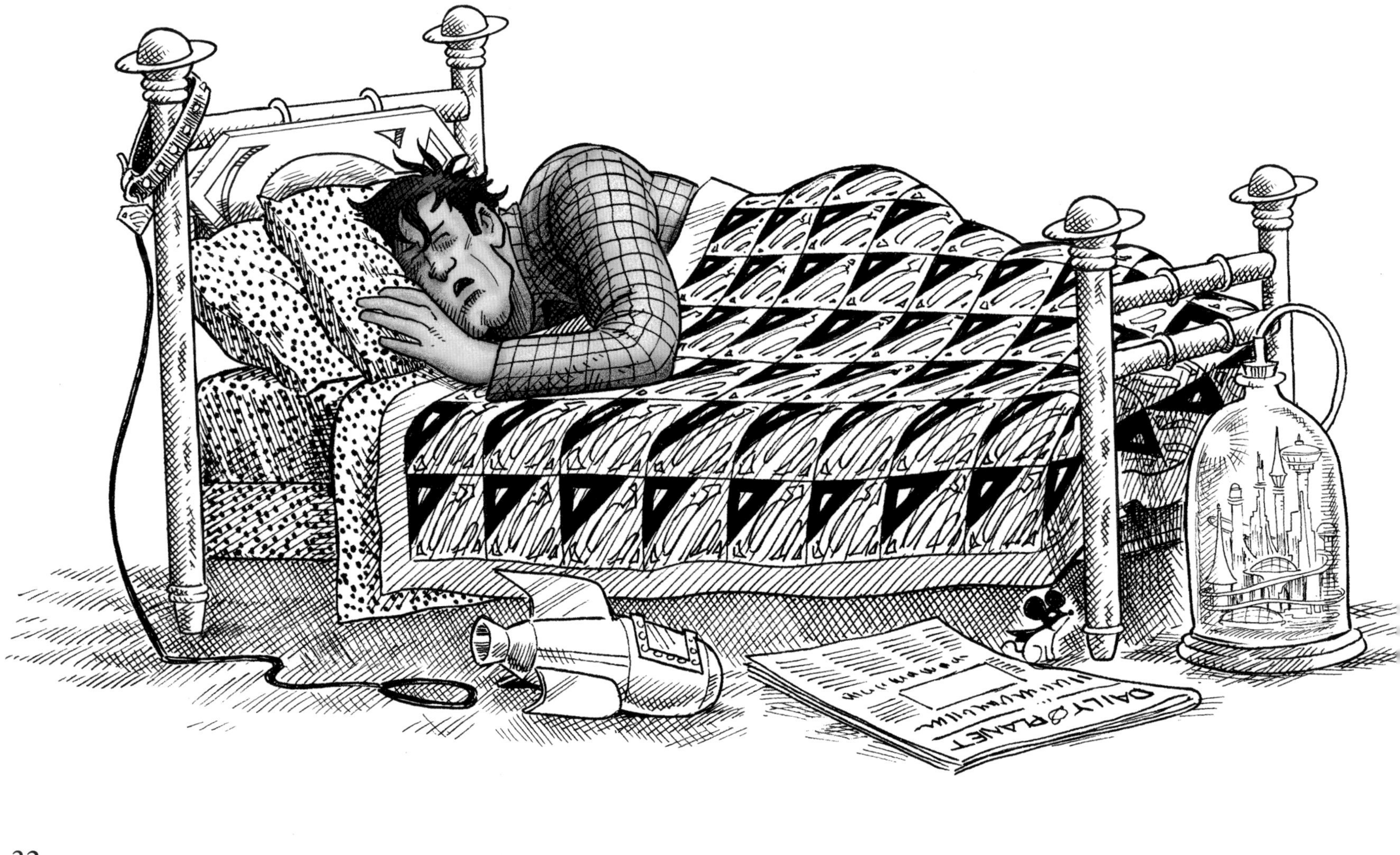
DAILY PLANET